BREAD WITHOUT SORROW

BeJae,
Rich beams when
he speaks of you, your
Iowa heart and songs.
I hope you love these
poems as much as I
love Iowa.
John Hodge
11/14/01

BREAD WITHOUT SORROW

POEMS BY
JOHN HODGEN

LYNX HOUSE PRESS
Spokane, Washington/ Portland, Oregon

Book and cover design by Joelean Copeland

Cover art by Charles Ritchie (American, born 1954), *Interior with Still Life* (detail), 1991, watercolor, graphite, and pen and ink on paper, 4 5/8 x 13 7/8 inches, Marsh Art Gallery, University of Richmond Museums, Virginia, photograph by Dean Beasom, © Charles Ritchie.

Acknowledgments
Some of the material in this volume was originally published in periodicals as follows:
Ad Hoc Monadnock, The Boston Review, Dark Horse, Field, Georgetown Review, The Little Apple, The Louisville Review, The Massachusetts Review, Poetry Motel, The Real Paper, Sahara, The Southern Anthology, The Sun, and *Whiskey Island.*
Additionally
"For a Friend, Gone For a Year," appeared in *Something Understood* (Every Other Thursday Press, Cambridge, MA).
"Stopping the Jesus," "This Day," "Father Superglues Five-Year-Old Daughter's Eyes" appeared in *Bone Cages* (Haley's, Athol, MA).

Lynx House Press books are distributed by Small Press Distribution, 1341 Seventh St. Berkeley, CA 94710

Lynx House Press
420 W, 24th Ave.
Spokane, WA 99203
and
9305 SE Salmon Ct.
Portland OR 97216

Library of Congress Cataloging-in-Publication Data

Hodgen, John.
    Bread without sorrow: poems / by John Hodgen.
       p. cm.
    ISBN 0-89924-112-3 (alk. paper)
       I. Title.

PS3558.O3426 B7 2001
811'.54--dc21

                                                        2001038032

for Doreen

. . . for thou art with me. . .

Psalm 23:4

TABLE OF CONTENTS

Part 1

Part 2

Part 3

I
moving heaven and earth

Upon Hearing That Among Marilyn Monroe's
Personal Effects Found After Her Death Was A
Signed Photograph From Albert Einstein
Inscribed With The Words "With Respect And
Love And Thanks"

Had they come together, beaker and bombshell,
like two asteroids meeting, like some big bang,
had they fallen for each other like twin Niagaras,
or perched like two cheesecakes on the HOLLYWOOD sign,
we all would have studied the sweet science of love,
shouted Eureka instead of Oh, God,
bliss would have blossomed above every bus stop,
until every man's hair stood up straight and unkempt,
and each woman's dress lifted up in the street.

All things are relative, theoretically,
and the stars simply wait to be named and adored,
but if there exists an alternative universe,
Alamogordo remembered or Paramount dreamed,
where God throws His dice in the crapshoot of love,
where blondes prefer gentlemen, where physics comes easy,
perhaps they are married, a nuclear family,
their children in labcoats and abnormal jeans,
Marilyn knee-deep in emotional postulates,
Albert all smiles, like the MGM lion, midriff bared,
their energies balanced in motion and light, $E=MC^2$.

Forgiving Buckner

The world is always rolling between our legs.
It comes for us, dribbler, slow roller,
humming its goat song, easy as pie.

We spit in our gloves, bend our stiff knees,
keep it in front of us, our fathers' advice,
but we miss it every time, its physic, its science,
and it bleeds on through, blue streak, heart sore,
to the four-leaf clovers deep in right field.

The runner scores, knight in white armor,
the others out leaping, bumptious, gladhanding,
your net come up empty, Jonah again.
Even the dance of the dead won't come near you,
heart in your throat, holy of holies,
the oh of your mouth as the stone rolls away,
as if it had come from before you were born
to roll past your life to the end of the world,
till the world comes around again, gathering steam,
heading right for us again and again,
faith of our fathers, world without end.

Stopping the Jesus

"Is Jesus Unemployed?" —Sign outside a church in
Gilbertville, Massachusetts

Just to see Him, you understand.
Maybe to ask Him where He's been all these years.

And if He were down on His luck, out on His ear,
on the road again, where crows sit on signs saying God is Good,
where semis go by hauling for Jesus and
shaking the air, maybe I'd go outside,
walk with Him for a spell,
the way my father said he would
before I told him he could go to hell,
before he up and died.

He lay with his face on a boiler room floor,
four hours before anyone found him, heart attack,
his sweat run off like children, his shirt unbuttoned, alas,
one hand curled before him like a cup, his back
polioed like a question mark, a giant ear, or
Samson's scattered jawbone of an ass.

I wouldn't want to stop Him, you understand.
You can't stop the Jesus. No one can do that.
Just to know if He'd seen my father, shook his hand,
if they'd walked for awhile, like Laurel and Hardy, bowler hats,
sons of the desert, another fine mess. I could live with that.

This Day

Today hell has finally frozen over.
Mephistopheles glides by, double-runnered, huffing,
spark in his eye.
Today God is getting new frames,
has lost count, momentarily, of angels and pins.
A sparrow falls, dusts himself off, spits, gets back up again.

Today is my lucky day. Heybobareebob.
I am plumb loco with luck, He Who Walks Backwards,
the one left alone in the wagon train ambush,
tetched in the head, maize boy, too much in the sun,
the one who holds on to the overturned lifeboat,
who crawls like a worm from within the mass grave.

I am high man on the totem pole.
I walk from the plane wreck.
There is no bullet that bears my name.
I will never be taken alive.

Today it is for other men to be broken into boys,
for others to saw at their legs to survive.
I am Jack-be-nimble. The world can shut its trap.
My friends, my brothers are the heavy hearts. The mark is on them.
They are scathed, fall chickens, good joes petered out.
They are the flies someone actually hurts.
No blood is daubed like unction on their chambered doors.
The man going through their rubbish outside
has brought them his sorrow, his vagrant plague.

Today the moon makes eyes at me.
Today I know the exact intensity that a woman brings
to the brushing to the left of the rivers of her hair.
When I hold her, the woman, the moon, I see in her eyes
the reflection, the waving arms of the dying and the drowned.
I wave back, lucky stiff, lucky bastard,
lucky as all get out and hell.

Procedure

This morning the crows have slept in,
fat judges in folded robes, so cold
even they do not know what to say, to pronounce,
from their chambered jabberings, their judicial branch,
from the sidebar hammerings of their haw, haw, haws,
about the endoscope, the lighted, hollow hangman's rope
that the owlish doctors, swallowing,
will push down my mother's throat,
the pale hands they will wash,
the centurion slit in her side,
the tube that will rest in her intestines,
stick in her craw like a worm,
like some tape come unravelling,
some gag order Roman decree come unscrolled,
some run-on sentence reading over and over,
you will live, you will live, you will live.

On Seeing My Wife Holding Onto Her Friend In a Parish Parking Lot, For Their Dear Lives And October Coming

Our friends, for all else that they are,
are this as well, the omens of our own demise.
They rise like Paul Reveres each darkened morning, rub their eyes.
They hobble toward us like runaway moons, or some mortal star,
to say some business is coming, some business is coming, some enterprise
of mercy or dying. We see them as if they are in the next car,
pumpkin-faced, stacked up at the light. We see them for what they truly are,
and know in their ails and ills, their headless horseman sighs,
what will happen to us, that heaviness we can only surmise
for ourselves. We see that we are growing old, that we are far
from perfect, that what has them up sleepless, what claws at their eyes,
what is coming for them, our friends, our hymn's amens, for the ties
that bind, is coming for us. We see their Easter Island heads, their eyes,
saying all of the truths we have known are now lies,
saying everyone, everyone, everyone dies.

May 6th

On May 6th, the Hindenburg crashed into the docking mast at
    Lakehurst, New Jersey,
and the clouds caught on fire, magnificently, the commentator saying,
    "Oh, the humanity,"
and we all got to see a mini-preview of the Holocaust, the Hiroshima
    bomb, the Atomic Age,
the Herblock cartoon H-bomb talking to the A-bomb, saying, "I'll take
    over now."

On May 6th, Louis XIV moved his courtiers, his attendants, his
    soldiers, and his servants
into the stately splendor that was Versailles.

On May 6th, Sigmund Freud celebrated his birthday, Anna, his
    daughter, bringing the cake
to him, gingerly, like a many-candled dream.

On May 6th, Crazy Horse surrendered, only to be murdered within a
    month at Fort Robinson,
and when his mother came to claim his body, it was delivered to her
    with his legs cut off
and stuffed inside the casket because the soldiers said he was too tall,
and his people took his body to the foothills and buried him there,
his warriors riding their war ponies back and forth over the grave, all
    night, slowly,
like in a shooting gallery, so that no one would ever find him again.

On May 6th, Randall Jarrell stepped out of a backroads North Carolina fog
into an oncoming car, leaving the sad-hearted driver for the rest of his life
with the first line of what could only be a poem about a man stepping out
of a backroads North Carolina fog into an oncoming car.

On May 6th, last year, a fourteen-year-old girl was swept up in a Tennessee
    funnel cloud
and was never seen again.

On May 6th, 1915, my dear mother was born, and now she is gone, and
    today I have seen her
again in the grainy footage of a video my student's mother made
of a poetry reading in a tiny bookstore seven years ago, me, jittery, jangly,
the new books lined up in the background like a fortress, a little Versailles,
    the camera
panning the crowd at the end, and there she is in her favorite knitted hat,
the coral-colored one with the pompons on the side like little koala bears,
and she is beaming, proud, and I play it over again, and she smiles every
    time,
and for a moment the Hindenburg floats, majestically, free of the tower,
    and Freud smiles
and lights a cigar, and Crazy Horse recites poems with Randall Jarrell, and
    the Tennessee girl
falls gently from the sky like Dorothy Gale to land in the shrubbery of
    Louis XIV's lawn,
and is not hurt at all, and climbs down, a little embarrassed, and joins
    everyone, everyone,
the courtiers, the attendants, the soldiers, and the servants, even the North
    Carolina driver,
still talking to himself, and Crazy Horse's mother, and the Hindenburg
    commentator,
for crying out loud, and little Anna Freud with the birthday cake, still lit,
and my mother in her koala hat, and me, even me, walking in the sunlight
up the golden road to Versailles.

On Having Been Given My Father's Footlocker, And On Not Having Opened It For Six Months Now

Enough, enough of your gaud, your guff, the duff
I have dragged through the leaves all these years. Enough.
Yet still you come, the floor dropping out, like dumb love again,
your hand to your head, rising like a drunken Gunga Din,
a stumblebum, dead to the world, queer on his feet,
a broken soldier, the light that beads up on the blood in the street.
Love, the hidden refugee, frozen in the wheelwell of the plane.
Love, my dear dead father, jack-in-the-box, up and at it again,
death's Ishmael, bobbing, the kitchen sink, an aunt
uninvited, umbrellaed in the rain.

                              It is we who haunt
the dead, never leaving them alone, pulling Lazarus's leg,
God's finger. The stink that we raise, driving peg after peg
through their hearts. What is it that we think
we have lost? Cities from our past lit up again when we drink?
Old lovers, hurts, the plans we have made? Our brothers gone off like deer?
We will meet again, the dead, the living, the dying. Have no fear.

Above Half Moon Bay, Near San Francisco

It is not quite grieving that I bring to this open place,
to the windy bluff that falls away to the Pacific, this aching water
that I thought I would never live to see.
This Pacific, that fifty years ago
saw the Yorktown return to San Francisco Bay,
listing, smoking, a gaping yaw encased somehow
in enough misshapen steel to keep itself afloat, to limp
under its own power, its men lined up on deck, unbowed,
in splints and slings to see their wives and mothers,
the workers by the thousands along the Embarcadero,
and the Gate, that comfortable span,
with the grand handwritten banner that simply read "You're Home".

This Pacific that saw the Indianapolis sunk
ten days before the war died down,
nine hundred lost, the survivors adrift for five days
amid sharks and dreams, the men so daft
with heat they dove to find the ship again
or drifted off, laughing, sure of an island nearby
where Betty Grable served sad tomato juice,
where one could drop away to bottomless sleep
to dream of this bay, this place,

where today a woman lives, a nurse,
whose husband stepped smiling
into an open elevator shaft
on an aircraft carrier construction site in 1944,
lingered for two impossible hours, a wreck,

spewing blood until, sheeted, they wheeled him away
just before she arrived, pregnant with his son,
who drifts now under the weight of his name
like a child swept off a rock by the surf,
who drives trucks each night along the coastal road,
and wants to work at the arboretum,
to feel the sprigs in his hands.

Below me on the pure white stretch of beach
that curves away beneath this ledge,
a woman steps out from behind these rocks
and she is nothing and everything to me.
She does not think of me here
and she knows nothing of the harrowed lives of these men,
how their hands lifted up from the deep,
yet she comes for them, for me, through fifty years,
gleaming, like a child, like Penelope,
for the light that lies floating on the tips of the waves
like a road on which, somehow, we can all go home.

Father Superglues 5-Year-Old Daughter's Eyes

*(AP) —A father is charged with sealing his sleeping
5-year-old daughter's eyes shut with superglue
following a fight with the girl's mother over money.*

So that she will never know the sight of love,
that stranger beaming, bright-eyed in the Joseph coat.
So that she will never hajj from those caves, the soft harbors
of those sockets. So that her eyes will never settle,
like pilgrims, like Moon's type on some dandy, some buck.
So that she will have to whitestick her way,
step gingerly past the stares, the chalk outlines of love,
the plastic-stripped crime scenes of husbands and wives.

So that she will never know love's subtrahend, its remainder,
the coins to be placed like lozenges on her eyes,
the stiff leash on the dime of her days.

So that she will be hood-winked, stone blind,
blind as a beetle. So that she will know Rosebud love,
Keller love only, like water through her fingers.

So that he can come for all of us
with love's mucilage, anointing, benighting,
waving us asleep, singing three blind mice,
cutting off our tails with a carving knife,
to see how we run.

Love Believed, Belayed

Once, in the doorless jumpseat of a Huey
that suddenly dipped and banked,
I slipped until my seat belt caught, yanked
me back to see, dully, fully, the screwy
open window of the world.

What had been dreamy sky curled
up (like a shade that lets go, that snaps)
to reveal the rounded tops of trees, a brocade
of broccoli buds, asparagus caps,
God's epaulets, the woods Grant Wood portrayed.

Then sky again, the world aright, re-made,
and I prayed the way men always have prayed
for the thing that has kept them from falling into hell,
for the tensile coefficiency of the metal safety clasp,
the second shift assembly crew at Belt Works, New Rochelle,
the mother's hours stitchers, the makers of the hasp,
the eyelet sorters, grommet bin boys,
all the canvas belt weavers in Heldin, Illinois.

Perhaps the world rolls over sometimes in its sleep,
and somewhere a lover falls out of bed, a rickshaw goes tipsy,
and someone falls more deeply into love, ever falling, ever deep.
It is only the world, this giant Rubens, this Van Allen gypsy,
peeking at the mirror of the moon before falling back to sleep.

Looking For Ophelia At The Former Site Of The Alice and The Hat Diner In Worcester, Massachusetts

It's still not safe. Your brother's dead.
Poor Yorick called. The convent's closed.
The nuns that have not gone insane are tied to rocking chairs.
(They face them toward the morning moon and tell them it's TV.)
No Hamlets anymore. Hardly a Horatio.
Algernon is dead as well, mousetrapped, Gonzagoed.
Kasparov has killed his king, thrown up his hands,
and wandered off into the deepest blue.
Everest is ringed with its everyday dead.
A woman swims from Cuba in a cage.

Cut your losses. Cut your hair,
Downsize, divest, go west, young girl,
to a place so small you could kick a tin can
from the sign saying WELCOME to beyond RESUME SPEED.
Get a job at the Kwik-E-Mart WaWa store,
the Piggily Wiggily Gas 'N' Sip.
Find a place where the chief of police is named Howdy,
where everyone has to share the same sneeze,
a chophouse hamlet, a one crow town.

Climb into the bedroll of heaven and earth.
Don't come out till the whirlwind opens the door.
Build the intricate city of love if you can.
If not, then come here. The economy's back.
I think we could make a go of it.
Some flowers in the window. A place to hang your hat.

On Carrying My Mother's Cremated Remains To Virginia Beach To Give To My Brother

I have been asked to step aside by airport security.
I have had to declare my mother's remains.
I have stated clearly and convincingly
that what the x-rays have seen,
what the slow inspector has delineated,
and what is as apparent as a child
in the grey-green light of the starlight scope,
are the grey-white ashes of my mother,
the dusty birds that were once her tender hands,
the one hundred and nine small white bones of her face,
their desuetude, their desultory grace.

I tell them I have her heart as well inside the box,
that I intend to hold it out to strangers on the street as contraband,
that to disturb that now would bring a terrible reckoning,
that I have nothing else to declare,
that I no longer have a mother,
that I am a dangerous man.

"It's All Over Now": Man Runs Into Texas Theatre Without Paying

I did not kill my lonely father. Upon my word.
I did not steal the president's brain.

(My father's heart stopped of its own accord,
a switchman directing a shunting train,
his lantern dropping suddenly, the kerosene
spilling out on the coal, blood pooling up in his brain.)

But I have killed the love I've been given, my petit dejeuner,
have placed a wreath on its grave in the rain, James Earl Ray,
have holed up, hinky, in a book depository,
love's Czolgosz, its childproof Tylenol.
I spell relief, wait for Guiteau, roll
AIDS off the charts, hit after hit, the next big story.
Man the Oz walled garrison. Grab the Johnson bar. Hard
to kill love now, the Lincoln
Continental shelved, Kevlared,
all bubbletops, Popemobiles, circled Reagans. You have to
squeeze each round. Hold her in your arms, this harlequin, this who-
hit-John, this stained glass window, gift outright, a tight
shot group. Jody was there when you left. You're right.

One can err in the taking down of love. Head shot? Baboon heart?
One can place the riderless horse before Descartes.
Stop me before I love again, catch her in the rye,

climb a bell tower, brave the stark weather, die.

I am the entry wound, Love Canal, glory hole,
the funeral train, buntinged, that rolls, will continue to roll.
I am the second shooter. I am the grassy knoll.

II
bread without sorrow

When my brother, punk-proud, d.a.'ed, alone,
came down the stairs, packed, ready, as always, to go,
and announced to one and all,
in a voice that shook and took hold
like a flag or shirts in the wind,
that he had signed up for the Army two weeks before
and was leaving now, right now (his voice hard then, tight),
we learned about hugging goodbye that day, that awkward gathering,
my brothers and I, numb, my mother gone crying in the kitchen.
As he walked down the driveway, stone on sand,
stood one more time under the streetlight,
lit a cigarette the way he always did
when he snuck out at night or ran away,
the red flame an eye from hell, roaring,
then suddenly gone, the house filled with quiet, close,
us all at the window like deer at the edge of a clearing,
except my father, in his chair all that time, reading the paper,
turning the page, snapping it into place.

My Father Swearing

Bitch, he'd say, always, when he could not work the wood his way,
bitch, as if there were a goddess of all his troubles, grinning,
a woman at the wellspring who skewed the nail, split the joist,
drove his hefted hopes deep into the ground,
bitch, his woe, his wound, his eldest curse.

And we would gather, hidden, my brothers and I,
huddled like shepherds by the door to the shed
to hearken to the litany surely to follow, the dam that would burst,
his power and rage, hammer and tongue.

Bastard then, predictably, and a marriage was made,
like an Adam come lately to a paradise of swearing,
the bitch and the bastard driven out of the garden
to bedevil him further, to beat the bejesus,
like a two-headed god, both mouths washed out with soap,
come to witness, come to share in the blame.

Then *son of a bitch*, and it all became clear,
a family, procreation, the Gilgamesh epic,
a new generation gathered against him,
and we were the children and he was the father
as he battered the wood, the precision gone out,
gone into the word, the word become flesh.

Then, always, incarnate, the rhythm established,
a flurry, a billingsgate of *bitch of a bitch*,
and *bitch of a bastard*, and *son of a bitch of a bitch
of a bastard*. There structure was born,
prepositional phrases, like blue Chinese lanterns hung out
beneath the moon, this swearing to God, this awful begatting.

We broke at that point, skedaddled, running off to the lilacs,
covering our mouths for fear we'd be heard,
to say in that darkness what was forbidden in the light,
a language mixed with laughter lifting up between the trees,
a forefathers' song, the words that made the world.

Dave The Guesser

When Dave The Guesser
guessed my age,
("Three dollars," he said, "within one year,")
he looked me right in the kisser,
past the crows' feet, the pent-up rage,
said there is no mystery here,
you've been on this planet for forty-seven years,
got it right on the button, didn't need the extra year.

Then he wouldn't let go, got a frenzy of seeing,
said he knew what my job was, my reason for being,
said my dog's name, the dead one, my brothers, all four,
my eight uncles, in order, even Bobby, killed in the war,
said he knew all their sweethearts, how they wandered alone,
said my mother would wither to wrinkles and bone.

He said I was the dark one, said my heart was a crow.
He said he used to know Jesus, said He's older than snow.
He said He's never returning, said He's hung up His hat.
He said he'd tell me where Jesus's hideout was at,
and that if I wanted to I could tell you,
for another three dollars. I only had two.

Room Service

The two men making love in the room next to ours
do not know that we are here,
so we hold what is in us, silent as flowers,
as monks, closeted, cassocked, out of respect, perhaps, or fear,
that what would escape would alter their joys, their sighs.

If anything, it would be laughter that would arise,
for what is in us is joy as well, dumb cousin to theirs.
So we hear their confessions, stare at the light in our eyes,
cover our mouths like children, mind our own affairs,
like a brother and sister hearing their parents go at it, absurd.

Perhaps laughter, not silence, should follow each act, each role taken on
in the heyday of love, the ballocky history that might have occurred
if Abbott and Costello had played Lewis and Clark,
Stanley and Ollie had herded oxen for free on the Oregon
Trail, hiding and seeking each other like two Chaplins after dark.

Perhaps we are always overheard, our yelps and cries rising now,
like Hope and Crosby on the road to the moon, to l'amour,
our love being listened to, audienced, attended somehow,
the moon smiling back, pulling the covers up to the shore,
our living, our loving, less lonely than before.

Jesus's Little Sister

How she loved him,
how she knew his road was paved to hell.

It was she, even before Joseph,
who knew that he would not be a carpenter,
who sat with him on the shavings pile behind the shop,
heard him whisper that the wood's blood caused him pain,
heard him punish himself in the woodshed at night,
watched him drive a slow nail through his hand.

She, too, who played hooky with him,
darted to caves to watch his experiments,
held them like pearls, like a secret language from her friends,
a feather from a sparrow he saw fall from the sky,
an earthen cup filled with watery wine,
the flicker from a dead dog's eyes by the roadside,
the first steps on the glittering moonbeams of the sea.

In the end she could not save him.
When he announced he would go into the desert
she gave him water, balm for his lips,
and, wordless, simply let him go.
In her dreams, always strongest on the nights
before some news arrived of his hell-raising, his trials,
she would know what she should have said,
that rich men can ride through the eye of a needle,
that they will butcher their own children for their power,
wash their hands of wandering dreamers.

She would say the dead are better off left alone,
that there is more than one way to skin a leper,
that Rome would have fallen of its own accord, rotted,
that kingdoms could be lost or won on a kiss.

One day she went away as well,
worked as a seamstress, her mouth full of pins,
her flawless faith in her thimble.
Your hands are a gift they would say.
At night she would put out her candle
with her thumb and forefinger,
exult in the little snap of flesh against flame,
dream again of seamless cloth, bread without sorrow,
of a boy who found God wherever he looked.

His shoulder, so pale, rounded, like porpoise skin,
the blue slipstream of the veins like worms underwater,
ganglions under porcelain. So at odds with the ruddy lower arm,
like George Washington's head on a Joad, Gilbert Stuart down on the farm.
This shoulder, white as pig roast, or trout belly-up on a beach,
that would leap to life, flip at my touch, my hand extended,
quivering to nudge him from the nub of his dreams.

Each time I touched him he would startle into speech,
a foreign foreigner, mumbling, murmuring from the place he had been,
like a voice underwater from some smalltown Atlantis
that would let him linger till he found his English, then lightly let him go.

For thirty years I have tried to wake him from the dead.
He will not budge, has gone so deep within himself he is a fish
slipping freely within his rib cage with his father, and his, and his,
ever smaller, always moving to forestall the days of convergence
when the biggest, lined up, can devour them all. They are dreaming as well,
(it is all they can do) of Grendel's arm, Arthur's sword, Thomas's fist
in the wound, the way fishermen hold flopping fat bass up for photos,
muskies and walleyes, pike and cusk eels. They are dreaming of Lazarus
steaming underground, yanked out once again, of Ahab's calling, fathers in arms,
Napoleon's hand in his pants, this coming to grips, this pulling at straws.

In my dream as I start, kicked awake in the night, as if someone
were pulling my leg, I see rivers of children tugging at fathers
dead in canoe bottoms, in the bellies of rowboats,
like mummies in hammocks, arms behind their heads.
And the fathers themselves are pulling imperceptibly at their children
without lifting a finger, hauling them slowly, from the shore, from their feet,
easing them smoothly, like fish over the gunwales,
past the oar locks, onto their shoulders, their piggybacks,
for the journey downstream to the mouth of the river
where the sun rises up round and white in the waves,
a god who has suddenly drowned.

For A Friend, Gone For A Year To Galway

Most days we will not think of him as often as we say,
time winnowing up, always, to fill the hollows in our lives,
the way we return from friends' deaths to our wives.
Most days he will simply be gone, overseas,
the water too wide, friendship slipped by degrees
to something manageable, an ague or filmy cold.

But some days there will be this tug, this hold,
a woman who left her baby at a church door in the cold,
and who stands now, watching, wracked, two blocks away,
or a man who scatters his daughter's ashes lonely in a bay,
the same man, comatose, who came back to squeeze our hand.

Some days, perhaps out shovelling snow, we'll note the bland
absence in the light, the day grown dim somehow, gone gray,
the laughter lost, the wit, the words all whisked away.
And we will look down the road as for a brother, again,
yet again. Sure, and we will miss him then.

Coming To Grief

When I think of falling insipidly through the ice,
how I pulled like poor Peter on Jesus's skirts,
clawed at the parts of the pond that still worked,
past the hen's teeth of ice, each breath coming out like a birth,
till I floated far-flung on the sled of the world,
I wonder, had I ended, bobbing, bloated, a buoy
on the dumb underside, wordless balloon, pinata from hell,
if my heart would have risen like a cold desperado
past my flailing third flash of family and friends,
my boots full of fish, my eyes two coronas, absolute moons,
my helicopter heart lifting up through the cracks
to drift through the trees, the silvery lace,
to your window this night, to your halcyon face,
to the home in your heart, to my resting place.

December

Another Christmas, no tree yet, no lights.
Another student holding out the dark lump of her life,
her friends lost, her darkness, a gift that she brings.
Then, in the distance, in what passes for a brake,
this clump of green trees amidst all that is lost,
like friends, like old uncles and aunts from the war,
men called Toddy or Nibby or Budge, women
called Chickie or Grace or Irene, drunks like Joe Hart
or Mrs. Paradise, and Lou Bishop the bum who once pitched
for the Bucs, all holding their own, lifting a glass,
all dead now, or dying. I miss them the most.
They knew they were lost, yet they held on for us,
stood like these trees alone in the world. This Christmas
for them with my daughters coming home, and planes
that continue to fall from the sky, and shoppers,
dead-faced, who are lost in the malls, their children gone off.
And this love that has come that I cannot account for,
this tree, this light, this place in the world,
this life I am given, this weeping for joy.

III
the breakdown messiah

Key West Cemetery, Mid-July, 2 P.M., Chance of Rain

Across from the heat of the Margaret Truman Drop-off Launderette,
near the Ninja Bar and the Shell Man Boutique,
where Hemingway look-alikes drone by
like so many safari-jacketed Santas on scooters,
behind the bent, locked, and rusted wrought-iron fence,
and below the concertina wire draped like sawgrass,
like sharks' teeth across the porticoes,
lie the dead of Key West, above ground, New Orleans-style,
mossed mausoleums, curved angels in love with their loss,
box graves, cracked sarcophagi, scrub brush,
an egg carton, yesterday's paper, detritus freely pressed against the gate.

Here the monument to the U.S.S. Maine, marker after marker
reading "Ordinary Seaman" and "One Unknown." Here as well
the obelisk for Los Martires de Cuba, a glass case broken through,
the Virgin gone, stolen, shards still strewn at the base of the graves.

When the workers go by, soundlessly, spent, in their truck,
the dust is so humbled by the heat that it rises only a little,
settles again, too tired to be anything else, dust returning to dust.

Past the trailers along Poorhouse Lane the warm voices
of the commentators announce the body count of Flight 800.
A two-engine prop lifts overhead. I mark it all the way for fear.
A man glides by on a rusted bicycle.
He goes so slowly and his eyes are so large
he is like the small wind that has run out of breath

and looks for a place to lie down. Fat raindrops appear,
singly, to splay like fossils, shadows of flowers on the cracks in the street.
Across the street someone has painted a mural of George Washington
standing in a boat filled with children, old men, a Rastafarian,
and a woman so at ease she can only be the artist's lover.
They are sailing off to another world, to a republic of dreaming.

We are old now, and our country is old
in its grief, in its hope and forgetting. Today bodies
that have fallen like rain, like the children of stars
in some slow war that only the sun and the moon understand,
are pulled piecemeal, in shreds, by men standing in cutters
beside the still waters, planes scudding above like mosquitos, like flies.
Everyone's eyes have gone dark in their looking, their loading,
their mouths opened slowly, lonely and separate,
the boats bobbing upward like headstones amid the debris,
the living, the dead like candles left floating,
like wreaths on the cemetery of the sea.

On Hearing a Young Husband's Testimony Before a Congressional Sub-Committee About The Manner In Which The FAA Crash Recovery Team Had Informed Him That They Had Found His Wife's Hand

Did they speak of it, the lonely hand, as a little plane,
turning it over and over in their hands,
noting its turbulence, its wake vortex, its aerodynamic coefficience?
How at odds with the other hand clapping,
its fine calibration, its full arc,
how it was designed to die, how it readied itself for the end
with its wear, its galling, its erratic yaw.
At the last instant, its tolerance,
its dampened oscillations, its loss of lift.

What of its moments, its movements,
holy and alone,
as it returned the folding tray
to its upright and locked position,
as it raised itself like a nightmare child
to hold her screams
when the cargo bay blew jagged, wide?
How it shook, her hand, and lifted in the sudden air,
in its final gesture, its denouement,
as if it were the hand of a student eternally raised,
or the one making the shadow of a fox
on a seventh grade screen
when the teacher's eyes were elsewhere, like grapes.

This hand offered up, this gag gift, this monkey's paw,
shall he carry it in his white shirt pocket next to his heart,
carve it into a wallet to enclose pictures
of the children he will not have, hold it out
to people on the street, saying this is her body
that is broken for thee?

This hand extended, this little home
(four lost sisters, a nun.)
This hand that rose each day of her life
to cross her heart, to brace herself.
This hand held out in lover's braille
to touch this space. This blessing, heaven held,
this church, this steeple.
This cathedral of silence and light,
magnificent, unspeakable.

Getting Through

Midnight, and the peeper tabernacle choir
is busting its buttons, beating the band, so loud, so proud,
it's a wonder we are not all out seated in rows, a proper audience.
They are singing hosannas in the house of the night,
because they can't help it, and because we do not,
another gift left unopened on the firmament floor.
If you listen even harder you hear the truckers' lament,
their high whine, their hard harmony on the road that they own,
harder still and you hear the song they are singing
to the one that they love even more than the moon,
the one who has loved them and gone.

I hear them this night, animal gospel, trucker chorale,
the song grown so loud now, like a train in the valley
that wakes people up on the other side of the world.
Already the five Chinese brothers are swallowing the sea,
and a boy and his sister are digging a hole to America,
their mother taking a nap, saying not a peep out of you,
the plump birds of Canton nodding in the trees.
The children stop digging once in awhile, whisper together,
press their sweet ears to the edge of the earth.
They hear a small girl dancing for joy,
for all she is worth, on the hood of a car.
The song she is singing they already know.
It is the song you hear now
in the heart inside your heart.

On Noting That The Most Famous Loch Ness Monster Photograph Had Been Faked

Tricked, jerked, chains yanked, nets come up empty again.
No pea-brained behemoth, no watery wings,
the shadows only shadows once more.
What was it that we sought, that blip in the reedy depths,
safe beyond time? Ourselves?
What had we thought it to be, our fears, our fathers,
fattened, clawed, snapping at us from below
as we skinny-dipped, shimmering, so many years ago?

Maybe awe, teacup-necked, ribbon-ribbed, phantasmagorical,
like cartographers' curlycued sea monsters on Columbus's maps,
the Niña, Pinta, and Santa Maria coming dangerously close,
like walnut shells, to the narrows, to the edge of the earth.

Or love, all our dreams gone out, bounced back off the cheeky moon,
phosphorescent, welled up in the tides, the bug-eyed, dopey grins
of a billion dead lovers, dumb as the centuries they left behind.

Or our sadness, closer still, reptilian, sunk so low
into withery caves, rising sometimes when the moon is in tears
to moan for us all and go under again.

Or God, barnacled, baleened, slipped out of the lock,
to give us our day, leave for awhile, let us sound,
breach, roll over on our backs, all of us,
mysteriously, deliciously, monstrously alone.

Garage

—for Walker Evans

Dead now, long gone, all three of them, the man in the slouch hat
    fixing a flat
in the single stall of his bay under the Cherokee Parts Store sign in
    Atlanta, 1936,
and the two women, waiting, would-be socialites, lookers, leaners,
one moreso than the other, fake-furred, harried, a luncheon, perhaps,
late and getting later. The other stands outside taking in the air,
warm already for March, the sunlight having traveled all morning
down the Mississippi just for her, the breeze from Texarkana come
all that way as well to nestle in the ringlets of her hair. She is for this
    moment
Venus at the half Shell, the hanging inner tubes like vulcanized haloes,
the tires her attendants, the spare fender her angel's wing.

The man fixing the flat goes about his business, moves with what he
    has, his steady grace,
the extra turn of each lugnut, the tapping of the hubcap tightly into
    place.
He does not look up at the women, knows they will drive away without
    looking back at him,
knows they will head to a traders' hotel, all hooch and hosiery,
    heartache
and hell. He works at his hands his Veronica rag.

He knows they will drive by again on their way home
in the deep blue black of the night, wine weary, worn out.

And he will be lying by the woman with whom he has lived,
with whom he is satisfied, who has waited for him, who has now gone
     to sleep
while he takes the last drag of his last Lucky Strike.

What he does not know is the color of the spot that is growing
on the side of his liver, that it too is blue black like the night, like
the spots on the floor of his garage. What he does not know
is the rain that will run and collect at the foot of his grave.

What he knows in his way is that something was in him
as he turned at the world with the wrench of his day, a thing
that was honest, his strength in the sunlight that crept in his bay,
the birth of the moment that was only his beauty,
his penumbra, like some part of a star that had fallen to a field above
     the river
and buried itself halfway into the ground like a seed,
still hard as the moon, still giving off light.

He knows that he has had this day, that there is never
any bringing of them back. He knows his garage
is his station on the way, that women waited for him
in his strength, that he eased their way,
that even as the warmth and the color left the day,
he has made order and sound out of shadow,
that his work will go on long after the sound,
the woman of this day, the man of this ground.

Hanging On

They say Sitting Bull, when he came to Manhattan
with Little Miss Sure Shot and Buffalo Bill,
used to ride the hotel elevator over and over,
Otis his medicine man.

He must have seemed like some Sherpa guide, piqued,
everything all downhill from there,
or some Gunga Din all gungaed out,
some gung ho ranger stuck in a cargo bay door,
refusing to jump, to say Geronimo.

Spirit house, he called it, the wickiup of ups and downs,
that lifted him to the vision place,
where Custer lost his footing on the Greasy Grass,
where wasichus fell upsidedown from the sky.

There that he had his greatest vision,
where he came to know that love moved vertically
(loneliness a horizon, roaming, always, prairie heart,
some Manifest Destiny relentlessly spreading itself),
love always rising or stepping off
the way one alights from a tram before it stops moving,
the jolt of love coming up from the street,
the way one ascends the stairs of a marriage,
steadying oneself on love's banister,

the way elevators rise in skyscrapers, past Harold Lloyd,
past old King Kong, hanging on, hanging on,
the golden doors endlessly closing, opening,
going up, going down, like our hearts,
forever plummeting to earth, lifting to heaven,
the sacred one, silent, inside.

Seven Crows

This is the moment before the song has begun,
when the phonograph needle drops like God's tender arm let out of a sling
onto the long continuing groove of the 33 rpm,
the stylus like a crucifix, rising and falling, like breathing,
the scratching like your father's voice talking in his sleep.

This is the moment when the homeless woman looks up without moving her head.

This is the moment when the MGM lion has finished the last of his roaring,
when he looks out at our faces lined up in rows and is satisfied once more
that there is no voice that will be lifted against him,
that the light will fade at the blinking of his eye
to rise again like a dawn.

This is the moment when the clothes of all the lovers of the world
are dropped, soundlessly, still warm, like clouds that have fallen to the sea.

This is the moment when the red-haired step-child is beaten,
when her breath flies away like a broken-winged bird.

This is the moment when the doo wop South African back-up singers
sing *ta na na, ta na na na* so clearly, so perfectly,
that they take over the song from the white boy fronting the band,
because they simply cannot help themselves, because they are in love,
because it is the thing that is in them to do.

This is the moment in the argument when the young woman
tells the man who has come all the way from California to get out,
and sees for the first time how much she is shaking,
and knows that she has never shaken like this before,
knows from now on that love will come for her this way,
cutting its heavy groove, relentlessly, stubborn as grace.

The City Of Rochester, August, Veiled Moon

Broken heart, busted gut, deep in its dregs and unending renewal,
the liar's song humming, loves me and loves me not,
concrete and sorrow, phoenix wings bolted to the top of the tower,
under which, in the ragged sleeve of early evening,
drunken men stagger asking for quarters,
sirens run constant in night's amber promise,
and wide-eyed young men tear down what was raised in the light.

Here men look just once in the eyes of another, channel their stares
to the pavement or sluices, and girls go in suits to jobs that demean them,
their heels drummed like hammers on the crosswalks and causeways,
back to sub-compacts, turbos, and radio love.
Here a trucker will be shot in the cheek by a man he just met
in the Log Cabin Grille, his rig stuck for weeks by the ramp to the thruway,
its carpets for Canada, fabric and pile.
Here a woman will throw her three sons off a bridge, leap in herself
and survive until dawn, raving for Jesus and the man who has left her.
Here Ontario County boys lean out of cars swinging bats at mailboxes,
laughing so hard they wet themselves, forget for awhile who they are.
Here Frederick Douglass and Susan B. Anthony lie wedded in death,
in suffrage and bondage, slipping freely in and out of the chains of Mt. Hope.
Here a woman ties her apron at 7:20 A.M., tells her shift boss she's late
because her children are sick, pushes fries at the ghosts all day
in the drive-thru, gives out game cards they scratch with their change,
the gunk getting stuck to their coins, their fingers.
Here a man all in gray in fedora and loafers orders Chateaubriand
like a critic of love, stares at a wall of Victorian mirrors,
its gilt, its duende, drifts to his room, to his robe and his ruin.

And tonight a young woman awakes in her bed,
one leg lifted up like a naiad, a runner, Mercury's sister,
mid-stride in her sleep. The sirens have roused her,
raised the four love songs, the lost sisters of the moon;
wanting, exulting, losing, and loss.
Tonight in her ripeness she knows the songs are all one,
and tonight she is weeping, and each heave of her heart
cries that love is a bastard, that he burns his own city,
like a barge set afire, set adrift from the others in order to save them,
the light swallowed up in the smoke and the shadows.
And she stands at the window, her breasts to the glimmering glass,
sees in the sheen what is there, what is already lost,
her heart's eclipse, her childhood hand raised high
with all the round answers to love.
And she knows love is both forever and nothing,
that it damns her and cures her,
that men will confound her, their claws, their eyes,
that she will discard them, look over her shoulder.
And she knows that most of her life will hold nothing that pleases,
that what chokes at her heart will torment and abuse her,
swell like a lump, a tear, a star, her heart a city
left alone on a night with no moon.

Letter To Katherine

Have tried walking (splish splash) on water, no mean feat,
bobbing, daring, perhaps, or just knowing, replete,
where the bodies are buried, the Florsheims shimmed in concrete.
I juggle, one eye out, one sharpened, on the balls of my feet.

Have heard suicide girl's mercurial lament,
between Scylla's canoe and Charybdis's tent,
have urged her to walk, cast her crutches aside,
alight on the refracted, polioed tide,
follow her natural summative bent.

And mumblepeg boy, how I've called him to speak (sweet-
ly), to shout hallelujah from behind the hung sheet,
to wax eloquent, to windbag, locute, to hoot
for the hat pass, the haul of the loot.

But he tells me she has fallen, in his guff, in his snoot,
sings his sad dipthong, water rising to boot,
the creek accreting. (And my toes, before long,
are dashaway, dashaway, dashaway gone.) For a song, a song.
I slog knee deep, one sheet to the wind, dissolute.

Then love (come again) in my ear, all around,
dead seas, dead bodies in a single bound,
my life in her inlet, my heart in her sound,
walking, unwavering, to her solid ground.

When The Cook Falls In Love

When the cook falls in love we can all eat for free
and the diner stays open all night.
Even Jesus comes in, the body of Christ,
bread and fish once again,
and water that turns into grigio wine.

The cook wants his lover to work as his waitress
so she'll call out to him, call him peaches or honey,
two eggs on a raft, one scrambled, one sunny,
two pigs in a blanket, two oinks in a stack,
two cinnamon buns, two stickies, too sweet,
one Adam and Eve in a garden.

He'll change the name of his diner for her,
call it Anna and the Hat, put in a new floor,
serve a Honeymoon Salad, lettuce alone,
put her name on the specials, Soup Anna Smile,
Call the breakfasts Anna Begins.

When the cook falls in love the world is his oyster,
some flavor he's after, some season he's known.
When he holds out his soup spoon he can sip the whole world,
say this is my body that is broken for thee.
And the world comes for dinner, sits at the counter,
spins on the stool and orders a round,
so famished, so weary, so hungry for living,
for the night neverending, for the diner of love.

The Girl Who Killed Her Mother Writes Me Letters

The girl who killed her mother writes me letters.
Each one arrives like some windswept bird in a world without trees,
like Noah's dove plumb tuckered out from looking for peace.
When I open the envelope, unfold the page,
I expect the words themselves to fly away, flit out the window,
align themselves on the telephone wires,
like some PTA banner over Main Street,
like Hitchcock's birds behind Suzanne Pleshette.

She says it's not so bad where she is, says they leave her alone,
says she looks at her hand sometimes as it curls around a cup,
says she worries about Jeremiah, the boy who hates his father,
worries about me as well, says she thinks I sound depressed.
She says she may be wrong about that.
She says she's been wrong before.

Men, Upon Hearing Of A Death

Upstairs in the cool darkness of the restaurant
women are spreading clean sheets
across a table.

The men stand outside in the driveway like disciples.
Each one has put his hands into his pockets.
Someone remembers an accident from the previous summer.
One man takes out a cigarette,
taps it six times against the box.
Another begins to scuff at a stone
with the tip of his shoe.

We are crows in a field turned to stubble.
We have become, irretrievably, our fathers,
standing by a doorway, silent as bread.